Let's Make a Salad!

by Frankie Hartley
illustrated by Clare Caddy

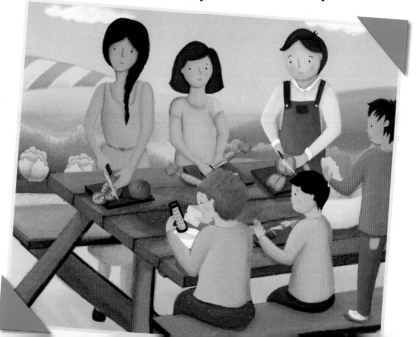

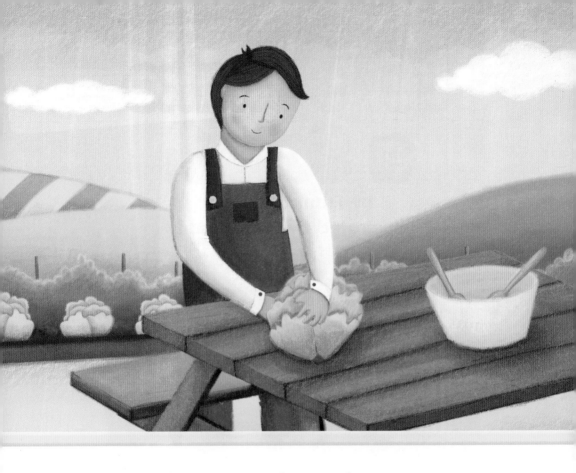

He gets the lettuce.

2

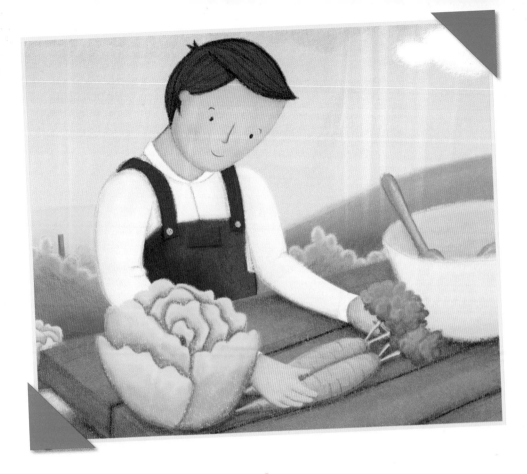

He gets the carrots.

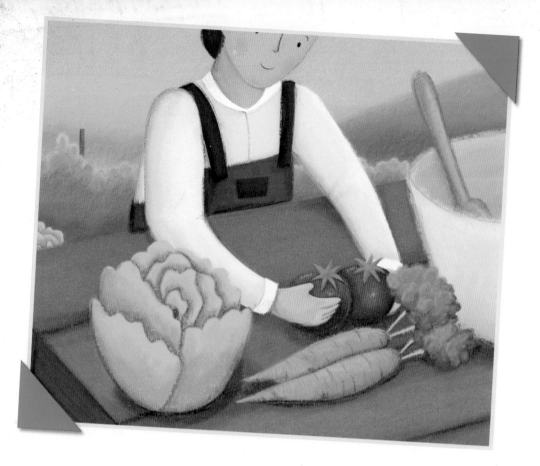

He gets the tomatoes.

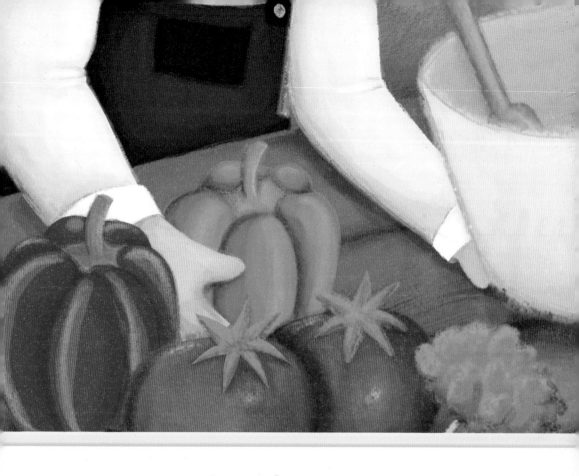

He gets the peppers.

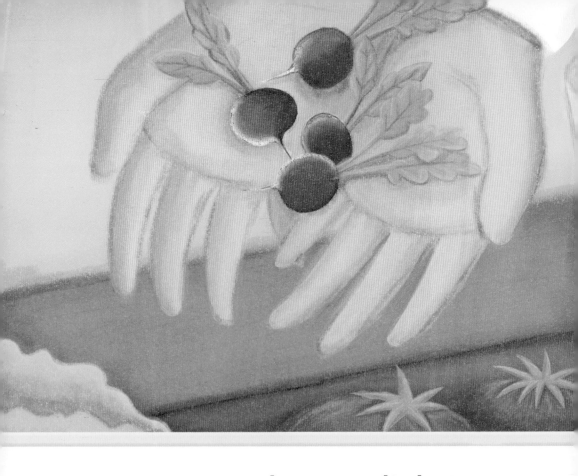

He gets the radishes.

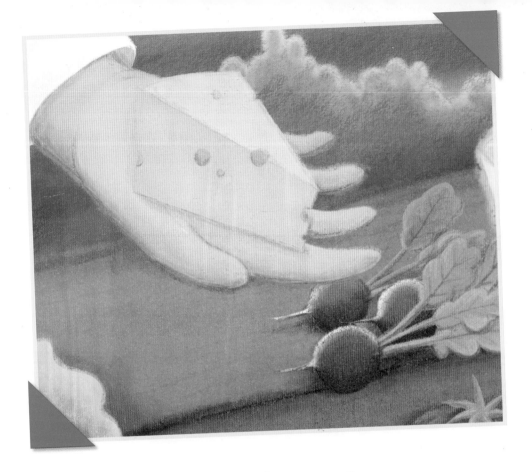

He gets the cheese.

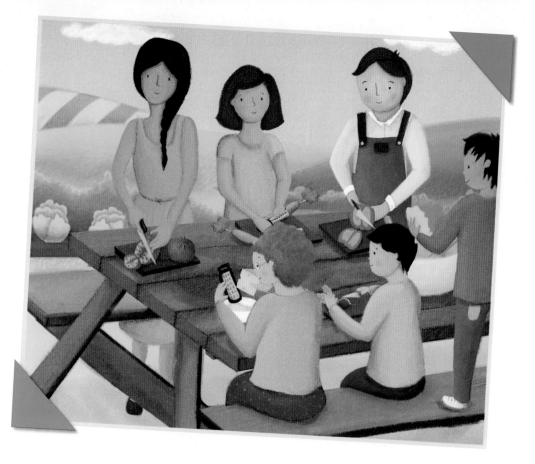

He gets the family.